Forex Trading

Ultimate Proven Guide to Profitable Trading

Advanced Trading Strategies

Josh Bright

© Copyright Josh Bright 2018 - All rights reserved.

The contents of this book may not be reproduced, duplicated or transmitted without direct written permission from the author. Under no circumstances will any legal responsibility or blame be held against the publisher for any reparation, damages, or monetary loss due to the information herein, either directly or indirectly. Legal Notice: This book is copyright protected. This is only for personal use. You cannot amend, distribute, sell, use, quote or paraphrase any part of the content of this book without the consent of the author.

Disclaimer Notice: Please note the information contained in this document is for educational and entertainment purposes only. Every attempt has been made to provide accurate, up to date and complete, reliable information. No warranties of any kind are expressed or implied. Readers acknowledge that the author is not engaging in the rendering of legal, financial, medical or professional advice.

The content of this book has been derived from various sources. Please consult a licensed professional before attempting any techniques outlined in this book. By reading this document, the reader agrees that under no circumstances are the author responsible for any losses, direct or indirect, which are incurred because of the use of information contained within this document, including, but not limited to, —errors, omissions, or inaccuracies.

Chapter 1 – How to Use the Economic Calendar

Chapter 2 – Economic News That Matters for the USD

Chapter 3 – Economic News That Matters for the GBP

Chapter 4 – Bank of Japan – What to Know When Trading the JPY

Chapter 5 – What Matters for the Euro

Chapter 6 – ECB and Its Mandate

Chapter 7 – Federal Reserve of the United States – Structure, Mandate, Role

Chapter 8 – What Matters for the Aussie Dollar

Chapter 9 – Bank of Canada and the Loonie Dollar

Chapter 10 – Interpreting the Housing Data in the United States

Chapter 11 – Bank of England and Its Role on the Pound's Fluctuation

Chapter 12 – News Trading vs. Technical Trading

Chapter 13 – Macroeconomics – How Investing Starts

Chapter 14 – Explaining Forward Guidance

Chapter 15 – Deflation vs. Inflation – How to Fight Them

Chapter 16 – Hyperinflation or What Happens When Money Dies

Chapter 1 – How to Use the Economic Calendar

This part of our series dedicated to currency trading deals with fundamental analysis concepts that are required knowledge for every retail trader. Central banks and their respective monetary policies matter the most in currency trading and, unless the retail trader understands what drives changes in the fundamentals, achieving success in trading will be difficult.

We've already covered some fundamental analysis concepts in previous books of our series. But here we shift focus to central banking, investing, macroeconomics, and other factors (besides technical analysis, of course) that the trader needs to consider.

For the retail trader, there's a strong temptation to only use technical indicators, such as oscillators and other trading theories, to forecast future prices. But it is said that while technical analysis gives the market's direction, the market moves for a reason. Working out *why* the market moves: that is fundamental analysis.

The Forex dashboard is formed by currency pairs that move against each other. Besides using technical analysis, traders interpret the economic releases for each country and trade the currencies based on their analysis.

So, we can say that trading based on fundamental analysis is mostly a matter of interpreting economic data. Some traders only use economic news as the basis for their trading-related decisions.

The idea is to compare economic releases from different countries and decide which one is performing better. Based on the outcome of the comparisons, traders buy or sell a currency or a currency pair.

The place to get economic news and be prepared for market's volatility is the economic calendar. No trading should take place if the trader doesn't know what economic release is up next, what currency is going to be affected, and what the forecast is.

Remember that fundamental analysis gives the reason why the market moves? The economic calendar will tell you why and when the market will move.

For instance, if the NFP (Non-Farm Payrolls) is due to come out, the market simply won't move until its release. Consulting the economic calendar is a good way to track the market timing and to prepare for the volatility spikes to follow.

The "economic calendar" is a basket of free information vital for everyone interested in trading the currency market. A simple Internet search reveals many websites that offer the information and the data is split into three categories:

- **Third-tier data**
    o This is economic news that doesn't really move the markets. Its role is to complement the other economic releases so that the traders can form a complete picture of an economy. Typically, for the economic calendars that use a color code to highlight the news' importance, the data belonging to this category comes in the color yellow, associated with non-market-moving data.

- **Second-tier data**
    o Marked with the color orange, second-tier data has the potential to move the market. Examples of such releases are the Durable Goods in the United States or housing data all over the world. These are

extremely important, especially if the actual numbers differ much from the forecast.

- **First-tier data**
    - This is where every trader's focus should be. Marked with the color red, these economic releases refer to crucial data for a currency or currency pair:
        - Inflation
        - Unemployment rate
        - Consumer spending
        - Retail sales
        - GDP – Gross Domestic Product
        - Jobs data
        - PMI's

For each release, the economic calendar shows the previous release outcome, the forecast, and the actual. Using these, a standard interpretation tells the trader what the market should do depending on how the actual release compares with the forecast.

If we use the unemployment rate as an example: the lower it is, the better for the economy. A low unemployment rate shows high employment levels, and an expanding economy. So, good for the economy and for the currency. If the unemployment rate comes out better than expectations (the actual lower than forecast), traders will interpret it as bullish for the currency and will go long.

On top of that, the economic calendar gives access to historical data as well, so that analytical traders can build models to see how the economy is performing now when compared with historical levels.

One way to stay up-to-date with what's happening is to always consult the economic calendar at the start of the trading week to see what news has the potential to impact the markets next. This way, traders can adjust the targets for their trades as well as improve their timing.

Chapter 2 – Economic News That Matters for the USD

With the Bretton Woods agreement, the U.S. Dollar took center stage as the world's reserve currency. It replaced the GBP (Great Britain Pound) and became the currency of choice when conducting international trade and the one used by sovereign countries to build up reserves.

It became even more important when the Nixon administration decided to scrap the gold standard in the early 1970s. From that moment on, the value of any given currency began to depend far more heavily on the behavior of central banking in the United States and other capitalistic economies. .

A new market was born, where mainly institutional investors could speculate on the free-floating currencies. Soon, the Internet and personal computers appeared, and retail traders gained access to the interbank market when brokerage houses offered access to it for a fee or commission.

Throughout all this, the U.S. Dollar's role increased in importance. A big chunk of international flows, as well as money supply maintained outside of the United States, makes the greenback the desired choice to build up reserves worldwide.

Even the Forex dashboard as we know it today – as we've discussed in the previous books in our series – is centered around the dollar.

Depending on the dollar's presence in a currency pair, it's considered either a major or a cross. The U.S. Dollar is the pillar of the current financial system and holds together the Forex dashboard.

There's a saying among retail Forex traders that if you know the dollar's direction, you know where all the other currency pairs will travel next. And what drives the dollar is mainly the economic news out of the United States.

As the largest economy in the world, it is no wonder that what happens in the United States affects the global economy. So, if there's one economy to study from a fundamental analysis point of view when trading the currency market, it's the United States economy.

Besides the interest rate decisions and overall monetary policy announcements and speeches, there's a plethora of economic data out of the United States that matter for the dollar.

Inflation, or the **CPI (Consumer Price Index)**, tops the list. It refers to the change in prices of goods and services in the United States economy over a specific period.

Typically released monthly, it is the data considered by the Fed when assessing the price stability in the economy. As a tip for retail Forex traders, the Fed focuses on the "core" release, rather than the classic CPI.

The Core CPI data doesn't consider energy prices because of their inherent volatility. The price of oil has a big impact on the inflationary outlook, and sometimes it is highly transitory.

For this reason, many central banks ignore it and focus on the core data. Another tip to consider when looking at inflation is to pay attention to the PPI release as well. The PPI stands for Producers Price Index, and it represents inflation on the producers' side.

The conventional wisdom is that changes in the PPI are eventually reflected in the CPI, which is why savvy traders watch the PPI. They'll have a warning about where the CPI is going to go.

Jobs data is second in line in terms of importance. Like inflation, jobs creation is a crucial part of the Fed's mandate.

Several jobs related releases offer clues to traders about what the Fed will do next with the rates. *NFP (Non-Farm Payrolls)* tops the list and is one of the key measures that the Fed considers together with inflation.

The NFP comes out every first Friday of each month and the price action during the NFP week is marked by tight ranges. Together with the NFP, the Unemployment Rate fills out the jobs data picture and helps traders prepare for the next decision concerning the federal funds rate.

Earlier in that same week, on Wednesday, the *ADP, or private payrolls* shows the state of the private sector. Traders use this release as a strong indicator for where the NFP will point, but there is no proven correlation between the ADP and NFP.

Initial Jobless Claims and *Continuing Claims* complete the jobs picture. Many traders view these as redundant, but the two come out weekly on Thursdays, and they do offer a glimpse into the NFP data.

The **ISM releases** come in a close third place. The equivalent of PMI's in the rest of the world, the ISM's name comes from the entity that calculates the rate: the Institute for Supply Management.

The ISM has two versions, each one referring to a distinct sector in the United States economy: ISM Manufacturing and ISM

Non-Manufacturing. Because the United States economy is service-based, the Non-Manufacturing (a.k.a. services industry) release is more relevant for the correct interpretation of the economic state.

One interesting thing about the ISM data is that traders/market participants interpret it relative to the 50 level. Any point above this level shows an expanding economy and builds a hawkish case for the Fed and a bullish scenario for the trader.

On the other hand, a dip below the 50 mark shows a sector and probably an economy that shrinks into recessionary territory and the Fed will start easing monetary policy.

Besides the headline (the actual number), the ISM releases a detailed report about the economic stance of each of the two sectors. For currency traders looking to anticipate the next rate change from the Fed, be sure to check that detailed report and not just the headline.

Savvy traders use this opportunity to check the employment component of both the manufacturing and non-manufacturing sectors. Because at least one of the ISM releases (and in some months both of them) come out before the NFP, traders use the employment component to predict the next NFP number.

Besides the ISM, general, standard economic data moves the dollar too. Retail Sales, GDP, AHE (Average Hourly Earnings), Durable Goods, Housing Data, Consumer Confidence, are only a few worth considering.

Even on the economic calendar not all of them are marked red, just to point out the fact that some of them are secondary in importance when it comes to moving the market.

Because the relatively recent financial crisis in the United States was caused by the housing sector, we've dedicated a special chapter to it later in this book. So be sure you keep reading!

Chapter 3 – Economic News That Matters for the GBP

One of the other key currencies that makes up the Forex dashboard, the GBP (Great Britain Pound) used to be the world's reserve currency before the U.S. Dollar's dominance. It has a long history because the British Empire dominated the world for quite some time.

The Bank of England, as the GBP guardian, is one of the oldest central banks in the world. It plays a central role in the GBP's valuation as it sets the monetary policy for one of the most influential currencies in the free world.

The United Kingdom and the GBP have enjoyed a special status in the last years. While part of the European Union, the United Kingdom chose to keep its own currency, and not to be part of the Eurozone.

For years, the two currencies (EUR and GBP) free-floated on the interbank market and the currency pairs they are part of are volatile enough to attract traders of all kind.

From the start, we might add that the GBP is a far more volatile currency than others, even more than the USD!

Pairs such as GBPCHF or GBPUSD have an ATR (Average True Range) much larger than pairs such as EURUSD or AUDUSD, making them an attractive alternative to traders around the world that have different strategies to approach the market.

Now that the Brexit has become a reality (in June 2016 the United Kingdom held a referendum to leave the European Union), the GBP and the U.K. economy deserve special attention. In fact, trading the GBP pairs in the two and a half years that followed the Brexit vote was news-dependent and a challenging task.

The United Kingdom's economy is a special one. Dependent on services, it's currently struggling to keep international business, after the referendum.

London is still the world's biggest financial district, with clearing fees outpacing even New York, not to mention Tokyo and other centers. The city of London remains iconic in the trading industry and generates a big chunk of the kingdom's GDP.

For this reason, one of the most anticipated releases is the **PMI Services**. PMI stands for Purchasing Managers Index and is similar to the ISM in the United States we just discussed earlier in this book.

In the U.K. the PMI comes in three distinct releases, for three separate sectors:

- services
- manufacturing
- construction

Traders pay close attention to the PMI Services release. If the services sector suffers, the entire economy suffers.

The PMIs are interpreted based on the 50 level, so anything above that level is good news. However, numbers too far above 50, i.e., 61 or higher, is indicative of an overheating economy, and the central bank can be expected to eventually intervene to change the monetary policy to cool things down.

For the PMIs the standard interpretation is that if the PMI beats expectations, the pound will rise. And in turn, a lower than expected PMI release will end up with a lower pound across the Forex dashboard.

The three sectors have different weight on the GDP, so it is important to understand which one is most relevant. For instance, it may be that the PMI Manufacturing release disappoints, but as long as the PMI Services still comes out on the strong side, the GBP will shrug off any potential weakness.

Inflation, of course, matters when trading the GBP pairs. The CPI (Consumer Price Index) release creates heightened volatility on the GBP pairs, with the central bank having the same target as all capitalistic economies: to keep inflation below or close to two percent.

What's interesting and unique is the Inflation Letter in the United Kingdom. It deserves special attention because Forex traders dealing with the GBP pairs must know when it comes out and why.

When inflation deviates from the target by more than one percent, the BOE (Bank of England)'s Governor is required to send an open letter to the Chancellor, explaining why this is happening and what the solutions are for the future.

Even more important is that the Inflation Letter release is followed by a press conference where the BOE's Governor answers questions from press representatives. Needless to say, the remarks create extreme volatility on the GBP pairs and opportunities for the speculative retail trader.

The **GDP** shows the total value of all the goods and services created by the U.K. economy. It comes out in various releases, and the most relevant one is the Preliminary GDP. The Secondary release rarely differs from the first one, and for this reason, it is mostly discounted.

The **Claimant Count** and the **Unemployment Rate** both show the state of the job market in the kingdom. The lower they are, the better for the British Pound, and the Forex market is the first one to react to any differences between the actual and forecast numbers.

Chapter 4 – Bank of Japan – What to Know When Trading the JPY

With an emblematic economy, Japan is a miracle of this world. Ruined after World War Two, it rose like a phoenix from ashes to become the second largest economy in the world.,

Despite its success, however, Japan struggles with a new problem, one far bigger and difficult to solve: demography.

With the oldest active population in the world, Japan faces a difficult economic time. The problem with the aging population is that the people don't spend as much money anymore as they used to do in their younger years.

Moreover, the younger families choose not to have children or to have fewer than older generations did, creating a shortage of people to replace the active workers. Obviously, the economy was first to see the impact and the problems reflected to the currency, the Japanese Yen, as well.

BOJ (Bank of Japan) was the first one to spot the trouble on the horizon. As inflation dipped into negative territory, consumption decreased at an alarming rate.

When the consumer doesn't spend anymore, or spending decreases, a vicious economic circle forms. Retailers don't sell that much anymore, so inventory levels rise. As a consequence, fewer orders are placed to wholesalers.

Wholesalers see their inventories rising as well, so they'll reduce orders placed with producers. At the end of this supply chain, the producers will have to lay off people and, as a result, the unemployment cost for the government will rise.

As a result, no one is happy: the population (high unemployment results in riots, discontent, etc.) or the government (deficits will rise, higher costs, difficult to respect budgets, etc.).

These are deflationary effects, what happens when inflation drops below zero. Or, more precisely, when the prices of goods and services drop.

To counter deflation and lower inflation, BOJ used everything in its power in the last few decades. Remember that the central bank has the same inflationary target: below or close to two percent.

It ran and still runs a massive quantitative easing program. Such programs, inspired by similar programs in the United States, were designed to bring inflation back to target, just like it happened in the States when Bernanke's Fed ran four separate quantitative easing programs in a row.

As it turned out, inflation in the States rose to target, but it's still falling short in Japan. Bank of Japan still runs the QE (buying JGB's – Japanese Government Bonds) with the hope that inflation will rise to target.

As a result of all this, **inflation** is the most important economic release to consider when looking at JPY pairs. Bank of Japan will do anything in its power to bring it back to target, even if that implies a total distortion of the Japanese fixed income market.

After inflation, the Tankan report is the next in line to affect the value of the JPY. It is a comprehensive report outlining the overall condition of economic activity in Japan, containing a detailed explanation of how the economy is doing at that one point in time.

Traders look at the employment component specifically and overall all other details that might offer a clue regarding what the Bank of Japan will do next with the interest rate levels for the JPY.

Perhaps the most important feature of the JPY and Bank of Japan's monetary policy is the indirect correlation it has with the global stock market and, in particular, with the United States stock market.

Because of the BOJ's efforts to bring inflation to target, the JPY enjoyed low interest rate levels for quite some time. When investors look for higher yields and decide to try to get them in the stock market, they look for money to borrow for trading capital or to invest.

Naturally, they'll look to borrow in a currency that bears the lowest interest rate possible. For quite a long time that has been the JPY.

So, investors borrow in JPY to buy USD to pay for U.S. stocks. This creates a positive flow on the USDJPY pair, the most liquid JPY pair on the Forex dashboard.

When investors take profit or exit the stock market, they need to pay back the loan, thus buying JPY to cover the loan. So it should be easy to see why the USDJPY rises and falls with the United States equity market, and especially with the DJIA (Dow Jones Industrial Average) index.

Chapter 5 – What Matters for the Euro

The Euro (EUR) is the currency of nineteen European states that form the Eurozone. For those people not familiar with how Europe is organized, the Eurozone and the European Union are two distinct things.

Not all countries that are part of the European Union have the EUR as their currency. Only nineteen do.

The Euro was born as the pillar of the European Union (E.U.) and has a remarkable story. The European Monetary System was born in the middle of the '70s, and the Euro as a legal tender appeared a couple of decades later after the Plaza Accord and the Maastricht Treaty.,.

Launched in 1999, the Euro as a cash currency began to replace the old currencies in member countries. As such, the DEM (Deutsche Mark), the French Franc, and the Belgian Franc disappeared, making room for the Euro as the common currency in Eurozone.

Today's Forex dashboard may be poorer in terms of the currency pairs that were replaced by the Euro appearance, but the Euro pairs more than compensate in volatility, trade flows, and importance.

The EURUSD, for instance, is the most important currency pair on the dashboard. It has the tightest spreads and the biggest traded volumes of all currency pairs. It should come as no surprise, because the Eurozone economies are second place in terms of their size only to the United States economy.

For the retail trader, currency pairs such as EURJPY, EURGBP, EURAUD or EURCAD play a special role because their volatility opens up plenty of opportunities on the FX market.

From a fundamental point of view, the **HICP Inflation** (Harmonized Index of Consumer Prices) is the first economic release in terms of its influence on the Euro pairs' volatility. Like its peers, the ECB (European Central Bank) has a mandate that focuses on inflation, and its actions are always aimed at bringing it below but close to the two percent target.

Messages sent by the ECB have the power to move the Euro pairs profoundly. Traders must watch the ECB speeches closely, and use Twitter economic feeds, for instance, to stay up-to-date with the rumors surrounding ECB actions.

Inflation comes out monthly, and the core values matter more for the ECB than the actual HICP.

Besides inflation and the ECB interest rate decisions, speeches, and press conferences, the **PMI**s in Eurozone are closely watched by Forex traders. There are only two PMI releases, and not three as in the United Kingdom: services and manufacturing.

What's interesting here is that the PMIs are released for each individual country, giving a clear picture of which parts of the Eurozone are outperforming or underperforming.

Next in line of importance are the **GDP** and the **unemployment rate**, and the ECB considers them both when setting monetary policy.

Chapter 6 – ECB and Its Mandate

As already mentioned, the ECB has a mandate to bring and keep inflation below but close to two percent. It is widely assumed among economies around the world that the two percent inflation level ensures economic prosperity and growth.

The typical ECB reaction to a drop in inflation is to lower the key interest rate level, or at least to send a dovish signal that the rates will come down at some point in the future. Because trading is a game of expectations, traders won't wait until the ECB acts, but will sell the Euro and the Euro pairs in advance.

On the other hand, a spike in inflation will trigger hawkishness from the ECB and traders will buy the common currency against other currency pairs in the Forex dashboard.

To fulfill its mandate, the ECB aims for price stability. But the definition of price stability is often a cause of confusion for many traders.

It doesn't refer to the Euro as a currency keeping a fixed level. Instead, it refers to the ability of the ECB to keep inflation at target. That's the stability the ECB wants to achieve.

The ECB's ruling body, the Governing Council (GC), meets every six weeks. Up until two or three years ago, the GC met monthly, but recently it altered its schedule, following the path set by the Federal Reserve of the United States of Bank of Canada which also meets every six weeks.

Interest rate decisions are announced on Thursdays, to fit in with the economic calendar and the announcements of other central banks. The decision is highly anticipated, as the ECB makes sure to communicate its intentions via a closely monitored forward guidance principle.

For this reason, the actual decision doesn't generate much volatility on the currency pairs. However, forty-five minutes after the release is made, the press conference is held, and highlighting any actions the ECB will take to fulfill its mandate and setting the course for future changes in the monetary policy.

The ECB has a tough job in setting the right monetary policy for the different economies that comprise the Eurozone. It takes guidance from the Federal Reserve in the United States, the subject of the next chapter in our book.

Chapter 7 – Federal Reserve of the United States – Structure, Mandate, Role

Since the United States ended the dollar's convertibility to gold (a.k.a. dropping the gold standard) in the early 1970s, the Federal Reserve (Fed) became the leading central bank in the world.

Setting the interest rate level on the federal funds rate is not an easy task. In fact, the Fed's decisions affect not only the United States economy and its citizens but also those in the rest of the world.

As the world's reserve currency, the USD is the currency used in most international trade. Furthermore, international loans are denominated in American dollars, and commodities such as oil have their prices set in USD.

It means that every Fed decision that makes the dollar either cheaper or more expensive will have immediate repercussions all over the world. For example, emerging markets are known for their massive borrowing of US dollars when the Fed slashed rates to almost zero following the 2008 financial crisis.

Now that the Fed has reversed the course and begun to hike the federal funds rate again, emerging markets are finding it difficult to repay their loans because dollars are more expensive. It should be clear that a decision in a different part of the world is enough to influence monetary policy, government actions, and population wellbeing in other countries and across continents .

The actual name of the US central bank is the Federal Reserve System and it has twelve Federal Reserve Banks spread all over the United States:

1. Boston
2. New York
3. Philadelphia
4. Cleveland
5. Richmond
6. Atlanta
7. Chicago
8. St. Luis
9. Minneapolis
10. Kansas City
11. Dallas
12. San Francisco

The ruling body is called the Board of Governors. Located in Washington, D.C., it has seven members nominated by the United States President and approved by the Senate.

Despite many people thinking that the Board of Governors sets the Fed's monetary policy, the reality is different. All Board members are part of the FOMC (Federal Open Market Committee), the body that actually sets the monetary policy.

The FOMC releases a statement on the federal funds rate every six weeks, on a Wednesday. Every second meeting, the statement is followed up by a press conference, where press representatives ask questions regarding the current and future monetary policy changes.

In recent years, the Fed has never changed the federal funds level at a meeting that wasn't followed by a press conference. For this reason, the volatility surrounding meetings with a scheduled press conference to follow is higher than otherwise.

For all the reasons explained in this book and the others of our series, this is the most important market event for currency traders. But the stock and bond markets, as well as regular options and futures markets, all tremble when the Fed decides whether to alter the interest rate on the world's reserve currency.

But what makes the Fed change the monetary policy? To begin with, it has one of the most complicated mandates in the world of central banks, a dual one. Not only does the Fed have to manage inflation, but it also has to create jobs.

As a result of this dual mandate, the unemployment rate and inflation together drive changes in Fed policy. The lower the unemployment rate, the better, and the closer the inflation goes to target, the better.

Therefore, the Fed has a tremendous job ahead of each meeting: to find a balance between the right inflation and unemployment rate and to deploy the required measures to fulfil the mandate.

Lately, some other important central banks in the world have started to question the inflation-only character of their mandate. As such, the RBNZ (Reserve Bank of New Zealand) switched to a dual mandate similar to the Fed's as well, , and Bank of Canada is also studying a similar model.

In all cases, the Fed is the central bank to watch for fluctuations on the currency market, and traders around the world struggle to understand the current messaging, as well as the Fed's intentions regarding the future path of interest rates.

Chapter 8 – What Matters for the Aussie Dollar

The Australian Dollar (AUD) is a darling for currency traders around the world. It has had a positive interest rate for a long time, a record superior to many other free-floating currencies.

That means that the AUD pairs have a positive swap, and this attracts investors on the long side. You should know by now what a positive swap is; we treated the concept in previous books. As a reminder: it is the interest rate differential between the two currencies that make up a pair, and can be positive or negative.

Charged at the end of the trading day, it diminishes or increases the equity in the trading account. Obviously, for swap-paying accounts, the ideal trade will have a positive swap.

Also called the Aussie dollar, the AUD is an important currency in the Asian part of the world. Since 1959, the Reserve Bank of Australia (RBA) has set the monetary policy for the Australian Dollar, known previously as the Australian Pound, due to the country's ties with the former British Empire.

Naturally, the interest rate decisions are the ones that set the tone for the AUD traders. In sharp contrast with the Fed and the ECB, the RBA decides on the interest rate monthly, at the start of the month, always on a Tuesday.

It makes the AUD extremely volatile, especially if the decision comes in the NFP week. That kind of week is difficult to trade as the RBA is due on Tuesday, the ADP in the United States on Wednesday and the NFP on Friday. As a result, many traders prefer to wait until the NFP until deciding on an actual position.

In the late 1990s the RBA introduced its inflation-targeted mandate, just like the rest of the central banks in the world. Targeting two percent seems logical, especially if one considers the period of high inflation in Australia during the late '60s and early '70s, with levels close to 20% eating away at people's savings.

Currency traders interested in the AUD pairs look at the **CPI (Consumer Price Index)** as an indication of what the RBA will do next. Sometimes, the RBA Governor explicitly intervenes on the market, as was the case with the previous Governor, Stevens. In an interview with a financial publication, he specifically asserted that the fair value for the Australian Dollar against its U.S. counterpart should be somewhere around 0.70.

At that time, the AUDUSD pair was trading well above the 0.90 mark, and traders were shocked to hear what the RBA saw as the fair value. Needless to say, the pair dropped in a steady bearish trend until the apparently desired RBA level was reached.

Besides the CPI, no other traditional economic data is that relevant for Aussie traders. Yes, the GDP offers a glimpse into the Australian economy's performance, but it rarely moves the market.

Instead, Aussie traders must pay attention to different things when buying or selling the Australian Dollar. Commodity prices and the state of the Chinese economy, to cite two examples, matter more for the AUD's volatility.

Australia has vast natural resources, being a net exporter of commodities around the world. It has one of the largest mining industries in the world, and its GDP depends heavily on the mining sector exports.

For this reason, it employs a lot of people in the mining industry, both upstream and downstream, as well as in related businesses, making it a vital sector for the Australian economy.

And guess which country is the biggest importer of Australian goods? That's right, China!

That means that AUD traders must have an eye on Chinese economic growth. If the Chinese economy is about to stall or fall into recession, demand for Australian goods will fall, and the first market to react is the currency market, by selling the Australian Dollar.

On the other hand, if the Chinese economy is in good shape, the path of least resistance is that imports will remain at least at the same level, if not rising, and that is positive for the Australian Dollar.

The problem is that the Chinese data isn't trustworthy. Traders should know that the Chinese economy is closely held, and data is not as transparent or widely available as in capitalistic countries. For this reason, one can never be quite sure whether the data release from China is reliable or not.

Moreover, the most important Chinese economic data comes out on Sunday, when the currency market is closed. It causes the Australian Dollar pairs to gap at Monday's opening if the Chinese data surprises in either direction.

As for commodity prices, gold is a good benchmark for the AUDUSD pair. For years, the correlation between the two financial products was so close that all you needed to do to trade the AUDUSD pair was to watch at where the price of gold was going.

In sum, besides the standard economic releases used to interpret an economy, Forex traders must have an eye on the Chinese economy and the price evolution on the commodity markets, especially gold and other precious metals.

Chapter 9 – Bank of Canada and the Loonie Dollar

The Loonie is the nickname for the Canadian Dollar (CAD). It is a curious currency, to say the least, with the most unpredictable behavior possible to see in the currency market.

It may be because the Canadian economy is fairly unusual. With vast natural resources and a heavy dependence on the price of oil, Canada built its economy on the energy industry.

Oil is, perhaps, the most important commodity of our time. We don't know what the future may bring, but looking back in time we can say that the last centuries' technological advances are due to the discovery of oil.

Almost everything we do today has a strong connection with oil. For this reason, oil-rich countries enjoyed tremendous fortunes and changed their economy dramatically (e.g. Saudi Arabia).

In the case of Canada, oil plays a central role. And because it shares a border with the largest economy in the world (United States), over 75% of Canadian oil exports go to the United States.

For this reason, the **oil inventories** in the United States is one of the most critical pieces of data that affects the value of the

Canadian Dollar. Everyone keeps an eye on the oil consumption in the largest economy in the world, from traders to the Bank of Canada and the Fed.

The Canadian Dollar, therefore, enjoys a direct correlation with the price of oil, because the Canadian economy is so energy-dependent one. The arithmetic is simple: lower oil price results in a lower GDP, hence negative for the currency, while higher oil prices are a net positive for the Canadian Dollar.

Along the same line, **OPEC (Organization of Petroleum Exporting Countries) meetings** and production decisions that affect the balance of supply and demand are also key when trading the CAD pairs. Put simply, any oil-related news or event affects the value of the Loonie dollar even more than BOC's (Bank of Canada) actions might.

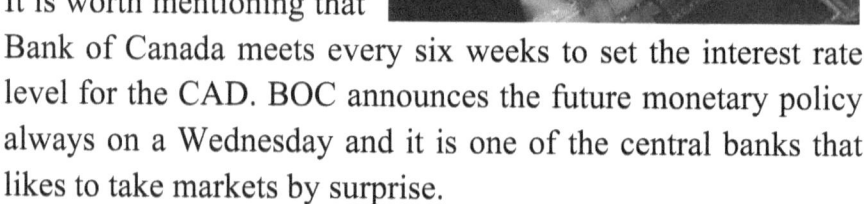

And now you understand why the Bank of Canada and its interest rate decisions aren't in first place when it comes to influencing the CAD's value. In fact, not once has the market reversed a Bank of Canada's decision on some oil-related news.

It is worth mentioning that Bank of Canada meets every six weeks to set the interest rate level for the CAD. BOC announces the future monetary policy always on a Wednesday and it is one of the central banks that likes to take markets by surprise.

This is something unusual in these days, as most central banks strive to provide forward guidance so that the market participants understand their intentions. Bank of Canada, while providing some sort of forward guidance, likes to deliver a surprise rate cut or hike from time to time, to remind traders who's in charge of the monetary policy.

Chapter 10 – Interpreting the Housing Data in the United States

After the 2008 financial crisis, no one harbors any doubts about the housing sector's importance. It is a unique sector that tells much about what's happening in an economy.

For instance, it is a saying that just by counting the number of cranes in a country you'll know if the economy is expanding or contracting. A trader that uses fundamental analysis to interpret economies and speculate on their currencies will find such information very useful.

The United States is the only major economy that presents housing data as a distinct piece of economic releases. In any other part of the world, the typical release is the PMI Construction, as in the United Kingdom, for example.

Any PMI is interpreted based on the 50 level, with higher values suggesting a sector that is expanding, and lower ones a sector that is contracting. Obviously, the PMI report is more than just the released value.

It is a comprehensive analysis of the entire construction and housing sector. However, few traders truly open the report and try to understand the full picture. Which, of course, is to the detriment of a correct analysis.

This is why the United States housing data deserves special attention. First, it comes in distinct releases, throughout the trading month. Second, the detailed reports tell the true state of the sector, starting with the building permits issued and ending with the houses sold or that remained in stock.

In a trading month, the first piece of information about the housing sector comes out seventeen days after the start of the month. On the 18th of each month, **Building Permits** reveals the annualized number of permits issued.

The focus here is on the word "annualized." It means that the format is the monthly figure times twelve months that are in a year. It projects future construction activity in the United States because obtaining a building permit is the first thing that has to happen when constructing a new building. Naturally, the bigger the number, the more positive for the USD.

Together with the Building Permits release, the **Housing Starts** show the residential buildings that began construction in the previous month. The release is closely correlated with the Building Permits, and traders look for a discrepancy between the two. Any anomaly is interpreted as a miscalculation and an opportunity to buy or sell the USD.

Existing Home Sales show the number of units sold during the previous month and variations in this number create plenty of volatility on the currency market.

Almost thirty days after the month ends, the **Pending Home Sales** release shows the potential housing on sale pipeline and is a good indication of the health of the housing sector.

All the releases together give traders the chance to form a solid picture of one of the most dynamic sectors of the United States economy.

Chapter 11 – Bank of England and Its Role on the Pound's Fluctuation

Bank of England (BOE) is one of the oldest central banks in the world. It dictates the monetary policy on the British Pound (GBP), a liquid and very volatile free-floating currency.

On today's Forex dashboard, the pound is the choice of traders looking for currency pairs that travel more than the average ATR. It is known that the GBP pairs like GBPUSD, GBPCHF or GBPJPY have wider daily ranges than, say EURUSD or USDCAD.

BOE has an inflationary mandate. We already explained in this book how the Inflation Letter works and what the BOE does when inflation deviates more than one percent from the target. The target, as we've said, is two percent, and is standard across all capitalistic countries.

Bank of England's ruling body is called the MPC (Monetary Policy Committee) and it releases the interest rate decision every six weeks, on a Thursday. It used to be a monthly meeting, but BOE followed the path set by the Fed and changed the schedule.

One thing to know when trading BOE interest rate decisions is that there is no press conference to follow the MPC announcement if the interest rate remains unchanged. In other words, all you get is the announcement that the BOE left the interest rates unchanged and that's it.

Obviously, the pound doesn't do much in such instances, and the BOE turns its attention to the Inflation Letter and uses that press conference to communicate to markets its intentions.

For a central bank that has stood the test of time, Bank of England transformed itself into a modern institution focused now on limiting the liabilities of the Brexit decision. Setting the monetary policy in such a difficult environment proves to be a challenging task, especially considering the GBP's volatility.

Chapter 12 – News Trading vs. Technical Trading

The currency market is so big that the size of retail trading is insignificant. Only about five or six percent of the market belongs to retailers, with the rest to institutional investors, brokers, commercial and central banks, and so on.

Yet, every market participant, no matter its size and resources, faces the same decision: to trade news or events that move the market or to use technical setups. Or both.

Naturally, the standard answer is that traders should use both news and technical trading. But this is more difficult to do than many traders like to admit.

There's a predilection for either technical or fundamental analysis. In the end, traders use them both, but percentages differ.

For instance, a news trader will always emphasize the fundamental side of a trade more than the technical one. He/she knows the basics of technical analysis, but the core of their trading decisions is fundamental.

The other way around works as well. Technical traders do consider news releases as potential reasons for market movements, but for them the decision to buy or sell a currency pair comes from things such as support and resistance, trendlines, trading theories, and so on.

Therefore, there's a natural split when trading the currency market and traders choose either fundamental or technical analysis to focus on. For most retail traders, fundamental analysis means news trading.

News trading has both advantages and disadvantages. It is a great way to make a quick buck, and this is why it attracts so many retail traders as everyone wants to turn a small account into a bigger one as quick as possible.

However, news trading is dominated by algorithms, robots that buy and sell the market automatically. These machines are programmed by quant firms and can execute thousands of trades per second, running sophisticated math computations when trading.

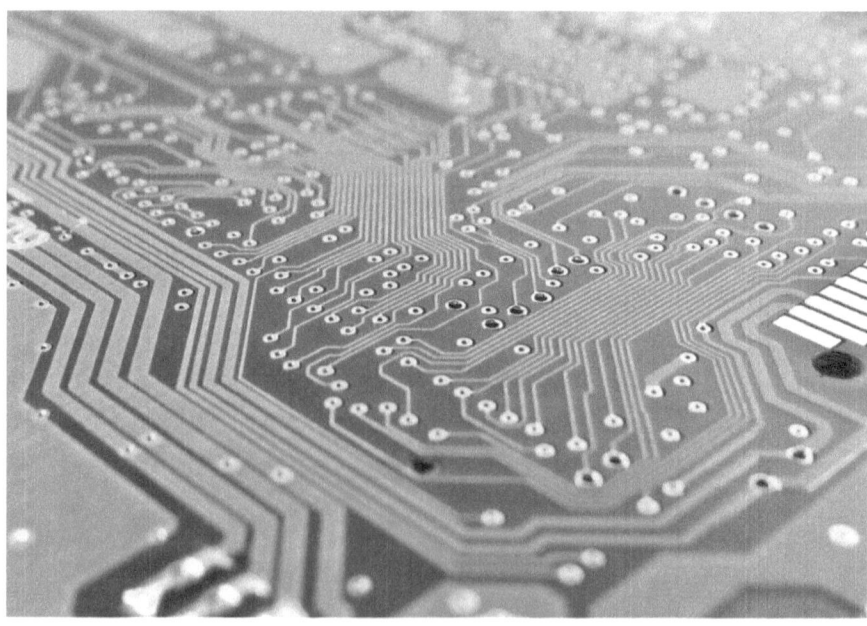

Ever wondered why the market explodes higher or sinks lower in a split-second when some important news hits the wires? It's because of the trading algorithms that buy or sell at the same time.

It is said that they are "glued" to the wires, in the sense that orders already exist to buy or sell a currency pair if/when something specific happens. The economic calendar that we explained in one of the previous chapters of this book is a great way to understand news trading.

Traders know in advance what the important events in the week ahead will be. Also, the previous and the forecast value are there.

These machines or trading algorithms are instructed to buy or sell based on what the actual will show. They'll act in the blink of an eye, and send the market higher or lower without notice.

A sharp move like this is both a blessing and a curse. If you are on the right side of the market, profits are made instantly. But if not, the money from the trading account simply vanishes.

When using news trading, the basic principle is to never gamble on a news release. Savvy traders wait for the first market reaction before entering the market.

They wait for the news to come out and for the algorithms to make the first move. Then, traders go on the lower timeframes such as the five-minute or even the one-minute chart and trade in the same direction as the initial market reaction when the market reaches overbought or oversold levels. Therefore, the smart technique for news trading is a blend between the trading algorithm's reaction and technical analysis.

With this chapter, we tried to illustrate that there's a strong link between news trading and technical trading and traders do use them both, despite typically relying more on one over the other.

Fundamental traders, therefore, do use technical analysis to confirm their thesis, while technical traders do use news trading as the reason why the market travels.

Chapter 13 – Macroeconomics – How Investing Starts

Time is the one element that differentiates trading strategies. Different trading styles are based on the time-horizon of a trade.

Scalping is trading with a short or very short-term time horizon, and traders use lower timeframes such as the five-minute or even the one-minute chart. Swing trading is when traders are willing to keep positions open more than a few hours and up to a couple of weeks and sometimes more.

A trader is Investing when time is not an issue. It doesn't matter WHEN the market turns or reaches the target, it is more a matter of being right or wrong.

Investors study the same economic news as traders using news trading, but they don't trade on the market move generated by the news. Instead, investors use the economic data and put together a diagnosis of an economy.

Typically, investors are early in a trade, because they always try to anticipate the next market cycle. Macroeconomic analysis is the process of looking at various economies in different part of the world and investing based on the outcome.

It is a complex analytical process that requires plenty of capital and patience. Macro-traders buy or sell a currency pair based on differences in monetary policies. If the market doesn't quickly react like it is supposed to do, that's not a problem.

The famous investor Carl Icahn stated that he shorted the EURUSD a few years ago at around 1.27 on the back of the Eurozone troubles, the ECB easing and the Fed not willing to move the federal funds rate below zero.

The macro-analysis proved to be right, as the EURUSD pair collapsed to almost parity. However, before collapsing, it moved first to 1.43, quite a distance. Many retail traders can't afford this kind of a headwind, but investors, again, have both the patience and capital to withstand such market conditions.

Value-investing is a similar process to trading using macro-analysis, the difference being only that traders using value-investing are active on the stock market, not the currency market.

Chapter 14 – Explaining Forward Guidance

Forward guidance became a de-facto monetary policy tool only recently. Up until the 2008 financial crisis, all central banks needed to do was to lower the interest rate level when inflation dropped, or hike it when inflation moved to the upside.

The process, called monetary easing in the first case and monetary tightening in the second one, was straightforward and there were fewer surprises down the road. However, once the 2008 financial crisis ignited in the United States, it became crystal clear that this was a global crisis and not a local one.

The way the financial system functions in the 21st century doesn't allow a problem to remain local, as the entire world had exposure on the U.S. housing market and on the U.S. Dollar.

When the Fed lowered the rates to zero in an overnight move, it eased conditions on the largest economy in the world and effectively provided liquidity to commercial banks under pressure. The idea was to stimulate commercial banks to take more risks and invest in the economy.

It didn't work, because banks were more concerned about liquidity and capital and were using their excess reserves, if any, to cover for their NPLs (Non-Performing Loans). But as it turned out, the Fed was quite an innovative institution.

Under the close guidance of Ben Bernanke, it began buying U.S. Government bonds in a process dubbed Quantitative Easing

(QE). But that was only one of the unprecedented and unconventional measures taken by the Fed.

The Fed was the first to realize the old way of conducting monetary policy was over. The world changed, economies changed, and monetary policy had to do the same.

One of the cleverest ideas the Fed had was to create a new system to communicate to markets. Because trading financial markets is governed by algorithmic operations, markets can collapse instantly if the communication process isn't conducted carefully.

So the Fed initiated a forward guidance principle, quickly followed by other central banks in the world, such as the ECB. The idea is quite simple: to better communicate to markets what the intentions are for the future and better explain monetary policy decisions.

Moreover, under the forward guidance principle, central banks also establish specific conditions needed for the central bank to take action. For instance, during the QE programs, the Fed used the Unemployment Rate level to signal the end of the programs.

In other words, the final round of QE was supposed to last only until the Unemployment Rate reached a certain level. Everyone involved in trading the currency market knew that, so when the Unemployment Rate got close to the target, the USD rose as the easing process was supposed to end.

The idea behind the forward guidance principle is to create less volatility in the markets. Whether it works or not is a debate, as traders quickly turned their attention to future monetary policy decisions.

In any case, one thing is for sure: since its introduction, the effectiveness of forward guidance has made it one of the favorite monetary policy tools, part of the arsenal to conduct monetary policy in the 21st-century.

Chapter 15 – Deflation vs. Inflation – How to Fight Them

Throughout this book and the other ones of our series, you've heard many things about inflation. It plays a crucial role in trading the currency market because central banks run their monetary policy based on the level of inflation.

Most central banks consider the two percent target to be healthy for steady economic growth, but that might change in the future. For now, it remains the line in the sand for central banking around the world.

Inflation refers to a rise in the price of goods and services. It stimulates consumption, and consumption is the one thing that makes an economy grow.

Here's an example. Assume you want to buy something, let's say a computer.

If the price of the computer rises, even a little, in a short period, you'll be tempted to buy it sooner out of fear of having to pay more for it in the future. In other words, you're not postponing the buying decision, and the item got sold.

The seller will place an order to the producer, the producer will start building supplies to manufacture it, people will have secure jobs, and the government has less unemployment benefits to pay. Not to mention people are happier because a growing economy brings high levels of personal satisfaction.

So that's the reason why inflation matters for central banking. When it rises over the two percent target, the central bank becomes alarmed. There's too much money in the economy, and the bank will start a "draining" process, by raising the interest rates.

By doing that, it stimulates commercial banks to stop lending to businesses and the general population, and simply put their excess reserves in overnight deposits with the central bank. For that, they'll receive guaranteed interest, without taking the unnecessary risks associated with lending.

The higher inflation goes, the higher the interest rates will go. But, as we'll demonstrate in the next chapter, that's not always the best solution, as hyperinflation is a real danger.

The example with the computer used here shows why a certain inflation level helps an economy. But what do you do when the price of a good or service falls?

Clearly, the first reaction of most human beings is that it's now a bargain and that's great for a deal. It may be so, but that's only on first look, and it's a circumstance you don't want to have for an extended period of time.

If prices keep falling, people will keep postponing their purchasing decisions – out of fear of missing out on an even lower price in the future. Retailers won't sell anymore, inventories will rise, producers will have to lay off people, unemployment will rise, and the economy will fall into recession.

When inflation falls below zero, it is said that the economy reached deflationary territory, and that's very difficult for central banks to fight. One clear response is to cut interest rates, but up until recently, central banks never dropped the rate below zero.

Nowadays, however, negative rates are a reality, and some economies remain resilient despite such stimulus. We can say, without a shadow of doubt, that between inflation or deflation, the second one is far worse for an economy and population than the first one is.

So, from this moment on, when you see the prices of goods and services dropping, think twice whether it's a good or a bad thing. Not only because it doesn't bring anything good for the economy, but it signals deeper and larger problems ahead.

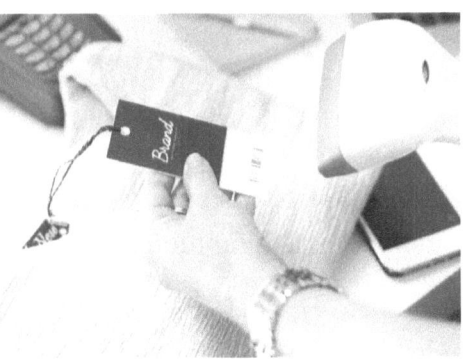

Chapter 16 – Hyperinflation or What Happens When Money Dies

As we get closer to the end of this book, we should finish with what money is and what it means to people around the world.

Money is one of the best things to happen to humankind. Because of it, we benefit from assistance in everything we do in our day-to-day life.

Think of it! You feel sick? You go to the hospital, and someone is there to treat you. Why? Because he/she is paid to do that, and the reason why he/she is there is money, not because the doctor is fond of you and would simply like to offer help.

Or, say you need assistance in buying a house, so you enlist a real-estate agency to show you around. For a commission (money), of course..

We can find examples, obviously, in everything we do in life. Money brought people together, it is the cause of unity in a society, and is a fabulous way to trust people.

Why do we talk about money? Well, trading is all about money.

We, as traders, are here to make a profit, to sell high and buy low, or to buy low and sell high. If traders do not understand what money is and its importance to society, trading doesn't make sense.

Many of us take money for granted. Money, simply put, is something one must have.

But a close look at the concept of money and the trust that comes with it, reveals a much more sophisticated issue. The trust issue is what brings societies together, and money is a pure reflection of trust.

What do central banks do? They issue pieces of paper (banknotes) and spread them around.

With that piece of paper, people go and buy things, trusting the seller will accept the paper. It is amazing how paper (in the case of banknotes) and metal (in the case of coins) are the pillars of a system based on nothing but trust.

I trust you, you trust me, and everyone trusts the central bank. But what if the trust is broken?

When trust is gone, the money dies. As simple as that!

When money dies, it means inflation goes through the roof. Unfortunately, we have examples right in front of our eyes, with some economies in the world facing terrible crises.

Venezuela, Argentina, and, to some extent, Brazil and Turkey, face tough inflationary conditions. People lost trust in what money is and fight hyperinflation with all means possible.

So, what is hyperinflation and why it is so important to avoid it? Put simply, when money isn't worth anything, that's the result of hyperinflation.

It means that prices rise so fast that the central bank can't keep pace with interest rate hikes. Venezuela is out of this world with inflation reaching a million percent or something close, and no one trusts the Bolivar anymore.

The crisis sent people flooding into the surrounding countries, with millions of people moving to neighboring Brazil, Colombia, and so on. Again, trust was lost, and that's the end of everything.

The funny thing is that the central bank can't do much about it. Look at Argentina in 2018.

Inflation runs very high, and the interest rate level exceeds 45%. That's not a typo!

While central banks in Europe, the United States, Japan, United Kingdom, Australia, and so on, set the interest rate level up to two percent, in Argentina things went crazy. Not as crazy as in Venezuela, but close.

The idea is that money, in the end, truly dies when the trust in the system disappears.

Why should Forex traders care? Well, for many reasons.

First, the Forex trader is the first one to know when things go wrong. Because the currency market is the first one to respond, the value of money changes first, and the people feel the outcome later.

Second, when trust is lost, opportunities arise. Savvy traders do know that each crisis has a solution, and, in the end, money won't lose its role.

However, the challenge is to have the capital, the right information, and the will to take a bet against a vicious trend. Which, judging against everything we've discussed so far, doesn't make sense.

We chose to end this book with hyperinflation as everyone has to understand the role money plays in our lives. And also, the tough mission central banks have.

It isn't a secret that many people hate central banks. They think of a "system" or "cartel" that manipulates the interest rates for personal benefit.

If there's one thing to take away from reading this book, it is the complexity of central banking and why it is crucial for everything we do in our lives. So before saying something negative about a central bank from now on, think twice at the implications and the responsibility that central bankers have.

We end this book with an image of the world's reserve currency in the 21st-century: the U.S. Dollar.

It shaped the way we lived for the last eight decades, and it will keep doing that for who knows how many years ahead. And is all because of TRUST!

Without it, money is nothing.

www.ingramcontent.com/pod-product-compliance
Lightning Source LLC
Chambersburg PA
CBHW030954240526
45463CB00016B/2558